★ ★

EXPLORERS OF AMERICA

De Soto
EXPLORER OF THE SOUTHEAST

MATTHEW G. GRANT
Illustrated by Harold Henriksen

GALLERY OF GREAT AMERICANS SERIES

★ ★

De Soto

EXPLORER OF THE SOUTHEAST

Library of Congress Number: 73-13917   ISBN: 0-87191-283-X

Published by Creative Education, Mankato, Minnesota 56001
Distributed by Childrens Press, 1224 West Van Buren Street, Chicago, Illinois 60607

LIBRARY OF CONGRESS CATALOGING IN PUBLICATION DATA

Grant, Matthew G
 De Soto; explorer of the Southeast.

 (Explorers in America) (Gallery of great Americans series)
 SUMMARY: A biography of the wealthy Spanish explorer who became the first white to cross the Mississippi.
 1. Soto, Hernando de, 1500 (ca.)-1542—Juvenile literature. [1. De Soto, Hernando, 1500 (ca.)-1542. 2. Explorers, Spanish] 1. Henriksen, Harold, illus. II. Title: Explorer of the Southeast.
E125.S7G73 973.1'6'0924 [B] [92] ISBN 0-87191-283-X 73-13917

OCLC
228010

CONTENTS

YOUNG CONQUISTADOR   7

SEEKING POWER   15

EXPLORING THE SOUTHEAST   17

THE GREAT RIVER   25

NORTH AMERICA

CUACHAYA
WHERE DESOTO
WAS BURIED
MAY 1542

MISSISSIPPI RIVER

ATLANTIC
OCEAN

TAMPA BAY
DESOTO LANDED
MAY 1535

HAVANA

CUBA

SANTIAGO
DESOTO LANDED
JUNE 1538

HONDURAS

NICARAGUA

PACIFIC
OCEAN

N

DARIEN

PANAMA

SOUTH AMERICA

EMPIRE
of the
INCA

o CUZCO

YOUNG CONQUISTADOR

It was the year 1519. A young man from Spain named Hernando de Soto stepped off a ship onto the soil of the New World. He was a conquistador, a cavalry officer. All he owned were his sword and armor.

He was about 20 years old. Before he was born, Columbus had discovered a New World that would bring great riches to the poor kingdom of Spain. Thousands of Spaniards, many of them soldiers, had come to the new land to conquer its Indian people and take their gold. Young Captain de Soto

came to Panama at the time when Cortes was

on his way to conquer Mexico. How he wished

he could have gone with Cortes!

Instead, De Soto had to stay in Panama

and serve the Governor. He was brave and

won favor. Slowly he gathered booty from

8

his Indian raids—mostly gold. He and a friend used this wealth to build two ships for trading. But then an urgent message came to them.

Francisco Pizarro needed help down in Peru. He needed men to help him conquer a kingdom even richer than that of Mexico.

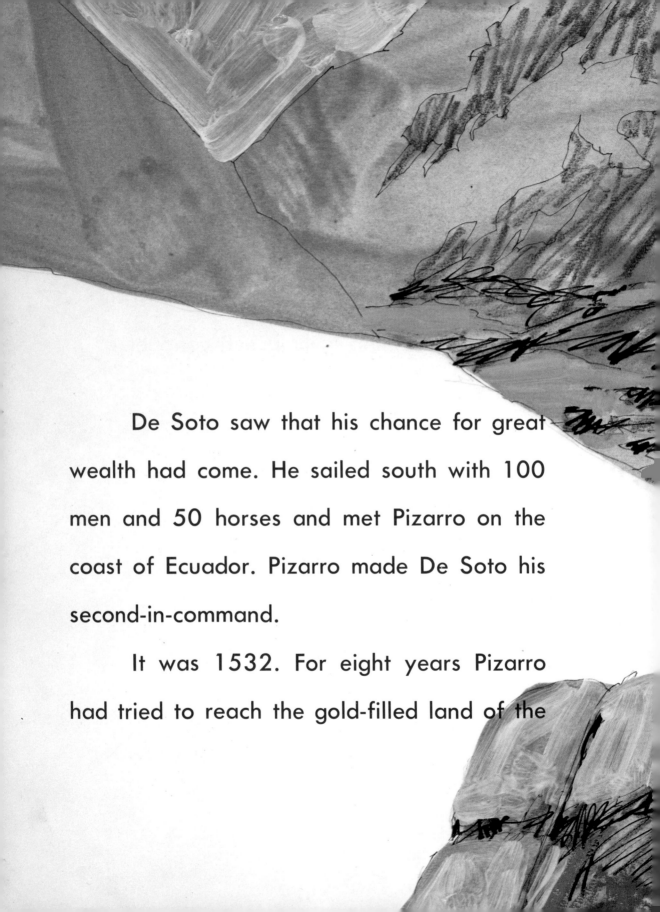

De Soto saw that his chance for great wealth had come. He sailed south with 100 men and 50 horses and met Pizarro on the coast of Ecuador. Pizarro made De Soto his second-in-command.

It was 1532. For eight years Pizarro had tried to reach the gold-filled land of the

Incas. Now, with De Soto's help, he was about to succeed at last.

The Spanish, 170 strong, marched southward.

They crossed the front range of the Andes. They came to Caxamarca, where the

Inca emperor, Atahualpa, had his army. De Soto helped lure Atahualpa into a trap.

Pizarro and his handful of conquistadors took the Inca prisoner and held him for ransom. Atahualpa gave them gold worth many millions of dollars, but the Spanish later executed him. Hernando de Soto returned to Spain in 1536, a rich and famous man.

FLORIDA

CUBA

SEEKING POWER

Money was not enough for Hernando de Soto. He wanted power as well. He married Isabel de Bobadilla, who was the daughter of Panama's Governor. Then he asked the King to make him a governor in the New World.

De Soto was really interested in ruling Colombia and Ecuador. But King Charles V of Spain was afraid that Pizarro and De Soto would get together and set up a powerful empire of their own in South America.

So he offered De Soto Cuba and Florida

instead, and De Soto accepted. There were rumors that Florida was even richer in gold than Peru—and it was said to hold the Fountain of Youth as well!

In 1538, Hernando de Soto, his wife, and a well-equipped army set sail from Spain.

They had 237 horses, fighting dogs, livestock, and all kinds of trade goods.

When he arrived in Havana, he set up his wife as governor. He sent some ships to scout the coast of Florida and find a good landing place. It was his intention to explore and seize all the lands of the Gulf Coast.

On May 30, 1539, he landed at Tampa Bay, Florida.

EXPLORING THE SOUTHEAST

They had 1,000 soldiers, horses, and a great herd of pigs, to serve as food for the men. De Soto planned to capture Indians as guides. But a great stroke of luck made this unnecessary.

An army patrol found a Spaniard, Juan Ortiz, living with the Indians. Ortiz had come to Florida ten years before, with another expedition. He was captured and had lived with the Indians ever since.

Ortiz became De Soto's guide and helped make peace with the local Indians. The Indian chief told De Soto: "There is no gold in this country. Gold is found in the North." So the Spanish army moved on.

The armored men slogged through swamps and crossed wide rivers. They sickened from mosquito bites and were bitten by snakes. Indians lay in ambush and shot them with arrows that went through steel armor.

Near the Suwannee River, the Spaniards had a battle with 400 warriors. But they fought in the open and this time the Spaniards won. Then they pressed on northward, still searching vainly for gold.

News of the invasion flew ahead of them. Indians fled from their villages, leaving behind the food they had harvested. De Soto spent the winter in northern Florida. His fleet came up from Tampa with supplies.

The next spring, De Soto heard about an Indian queen who lived toward the east. It was said she had gold! The army marched into Georgia. They found the queen—but her

"gold" was only copper.

   Disappointed, they pressed on into
South Carolina. Then they turned northwest
and probably passed through part of North

Carolina and Tennessee. Then they went southward again, into Alabama.

Men had died of sickness and in fights with the Indians. Some foot-soldiers deserted the army and went off to live with friendly tribes. In Fall, 1540 De Soto entered the land of the powerful Choctaw tribe.

These fierce Indians decided to stop the invaders. At a large Indian city named Movilla, De Soto and his army were trapped. They

fought valiantly against overwhelming numbers of Indians. Finally, by setting the town on fire, the Spaniards won. But they had lost many of their men and almost all of their equipment.

De Soto's men urged him to march to the coast, to go home. But he would not give up his dream.

THE GREAT RIVER

All winter, they traveled northwest, growing more ragged with each mile. On May 8, 1541, they came to the bank of a gigantic river. De Soto said: "We will call it Rio Grande." It was the Mississippi.

The mighty river was two miles wide but De Soto insisted they must cross it. They built barges. A fleet of Indian canoes came to investigate, but the army was able to drive them away.

De Soto now led his dwindling force
into Arkansas. He asked about gold. But the
Indians always told him it was to be found
farther on.

So they kept marching.

In the spring of 1542, De Soto decided to return to the sea. Only about 300 men and 40 horses were left. His guide, Juan Ortiz, had died. They came again to the banks of the mighty river, the Mississippi. And there Hernando de Soto fell ill—perhaps of malaria, perhaps of fatigue and disappointment. He died on May 21.

His men, fearful that the Indians would dig up his body, buried him in the river he had discovered.

Then the remnant of the conquistador's army went southwest into Texas, hoping to reach Mexico. They were stopped by deserts and turned back to the river.

In December, 1542 they reached the Mississippi. There they built crude ships to take them downstream.

On September 10, 1543 they reached a Spanish settlement in Mexico. Of the original army, 311 men returned alive.

★ ★

GALLERY OF GREAT AMERICANS SERIES

★ ★

INDIANS OF AMERICA
- GERONIMO
- CRAZY HORSE
- CHIEF JOSEPH
- PONTIAC
- SQUANTO
- OSCEOLA

EXPLORERS OF AMERICA
- COLUMBUS
- LEIF ERICSON
- DeSOTO
- LEWIS AND CLARK
- CHAMPLAIN
- CORONADO

FRONTIERSMEN OF AMERICA
- DANIEL BOONE
- BUFFALO BILL
- JIM BRIDGER
- FRANCIS MARION
- DAVY CROCKETT
- KIT CARSON

WAR HEROES OF AMERICA
- JOHN PAUL JONES
- PAUL REVERE
- ROBERT E. LEE
- ULYSSES S. GRANT
- SAM HOUSTON
- LAFAYETTE

WOMEN OF AMERICA
- CLARA BARTON
- JANE ADDAMS
- ELIZABETH BLACKWELL
- HARRIET TUBMAN
- SUSAN B. ANTHONY
- DOLLEY MADISON

★ ★